NORTHAMPTONSHIRE VOL II

Edited by Annabel Cook

First published in Great Britain in 2003 by
YOUNG WRITERS
Remus House,
Coltsfoot Drive,
Peterborough, PE2 9JX
Telephone (01733) 890066

SB ISBN 1 84460 261 3

FOREWORD

Young Writers was established in 1991 as a foundation for promoting the reading and writing of poetry amongst children and young adults. Today it continues this quest and proceeds to nurture and guide the writing talents of today's youth.

From this year's competition Young Writers is proud to present a showcase of the best poetic talent from across the UK. Each hand-picked poem has been carefully chosen from over 66,000 'Hullabaloo!' entries to be published in this, our eleventh primary school series.

This year in particular we have been wholeheartedly impressed with the quality of entries received. The thought, effort, imagination and hard work put into each poem impressed us all and once again the task of editing was a difficult but enjoyable experience.

We hope you are as pleased as we are with the final selection and that you and your family will continue to be entertained with *Hullabaloo! Northamptonshire Vol II* for many years to come.

CONTENTS

Charlotte Whiteley (10)	19
Harry Adams (10)	20
James Bevington (10)	21
Katie Wilson (10)	22
Henry Spencer (9)	22

Braunston CE Primary School

Joshua Tokley (9)	23
Sam Penhall (10)	23
Robbie Bunn (9)	24
Edward Gilbert (10)	24
Jordan Childs (11)	25
Bethany Whitlow (9)	25
Thomas Hill (10)	26
Laura Cooper (10)	26
Sarah Iland (9)	27
Emma Gibson (10)	27
Katrina Edwards (10)	28
Justin Boneham (10)	28
Jordan Hearn (10)	29
Jonathan Westall (9)	29
William Haynes (11)	30
Benjamin Lord (9)	30
Marcus Banks (10)	31
Oliver Lloyd-Wright (10)	31
Kelly Ford (10)	32
Tobias Underwood (10)	32
Poppy Anne Simmons (10)	33
Shane Davis (10)	33
Rebecca Cox (11)	34
Sarah Green (10)	34
Alexandria Natasha Hart (11)	35
Joshua Sullivan (8)	36
Chanelle Aspinwall (10)	36
Rebecca Broadley (10)	37
Danielle Childs (11)	38
Kallum John Bell (10)	38
Marisa Harrison (10)	39

Miriam Noor (8)	73
Ricky Jones (8)	73
Laura Dyson (10)	74
Jack Reesby (8)	74
Megan-Jade Hall (9)	75
Alexander Lee (8)	75
Harry Caulton (8)	76
Shane Sutton (9)	76
Georgina Bryers (8)	77
Adam Creaney (8)	77
Bronwen Edwards (9)	78
James Moore (9)	78
Amy Pow (9)	79
Shannon Craig (8)	79
Corina Staires (8)	80
Rebecca Pucci (8)	80
Shannen Brown (10)	81
Bronte Coates (7)	81
Monica Barmby (10)	82
Rebekah Fenwick (8)	82
Peter Gardner (11)	83
Matthew Langlands	83
Ashley Newell (10)	84
Jake Tebbutt	84
Amelia Spalding (10)	85
Jo-Ann Goacher (11)	85
Kayleigh Muller (9)	86
Chloe Stephenson (9)	86
Rebecca Wade (10)	87
Amie Billson (9)	88
Matthew Humphreys (10)	89
Kimberley Miller (9)	90
Chelsea Thompson (9)	91
Louise Dyson (10)	92
Kieran Cherry (9)	92
Jonathan Lane (10)	93
Jodie Bunting	93
Lauren Aris (8)	94

Karen Claydon (9)	94
Jordan Timson (10)	95
Stuart Jaeckel (10)	96
Joe Osborne (9)	96
Georgina Davies (10)	97
Robert Claydon (7)	97
Shauna Middleton (10)	98
Hayley Duncan (8)	98
Fiona McCance (10)	99
Tabitha Coates (8)	99
Emma Furnivall (8)	100
Ryan James (7)	100
Georgia Wilson (8)	101
Alex Kibblewhite (7)	101
Scott Smith (10)	102
Shannon Thompson (11)	102
Rhianne Wykes (11)	103
Tessa Withall (11)	103

Earls Barton Junior School
Stuart Maxwell (10)	104
Sam Homer (10)	105

Great Addington CE Primary School
Joanne Taylor (10)	106
Alex Page (10)	106
Charlotte Evans (10)	107
Naomi Brown (9)	107
Jamie Vendy (11)	107
Annabelle Chang (10)	108
Chloe Brudenell (10)	108
Antonia Brown (11)	109
Esther Allen (10)	109
Jonathan Bowater (10)	110

Long Buckby Junior School
Stephanie Langford (9)	111
Mary-Anne Blowman (9)	111

The Poems

THE WINTER WOLF

As the gusts strike like movements of whiplash
A silver glistens in the moonlight
The scowl of a dark figure calls over the land
As darkness fills the sky

As the blizzards cage and the blades of grass sway violently
The sound of a thunderous roar echoes through the vast valley
His soul is of brimstone and heart is of cold fire
And his piercing red eyes glare into your soul with passion and hatred

His coat glints, hiding the sorrow of the animal beneath
As winter's air comes calling
The hint of scarlet lies in his eyes
And the breeze is one of his senses

He dashes as if he's thunder, inspiring a glint of light
His granite-like claws glimmer, like a crystal lagoon
For he is the winter wolf
Consuming winter's continuous bloom.

Tom Barker (11)
Barton Seagrave Primary School

LOST TICKET

I went to Australia
To watch the cricket
Bought myself a first class cricket ticket
Then a man went and nicked it
He threw it in the darkest pit
So I didn't get to see the cricket.

Richard Bird (10)
Barton Seagrave Primary School

MY SISTER

She is kind, helpful,
Loving and caring,
She helps me with my homework,
Even when I'm feeling down,
She's always there for me,
When the day ends
She always puts me to bed
And I'll never stop loving my big sister ever again!

Olivia Steele (10)
Barton Seagrave Primary School

MY CAT, FRANKY

My cat, Franky
Is very manky
He eats a lot
And lives in a pot

My cat, Franky
Is a bit lanky
He eats lots of bugs
And hides under rugs

My cat, Franky
Is very shanky
He chases dogs
And falls in bogs.

Jake Parker (10)
Barton Seagrave Primary School

MY PET SNAKE

My pet snake
Is as long as a rake
It slithers and slides
And always hides
It eats dead rats
And squashy bats
His home is very warm and cosy
Even though his neighbours are nosy
They stop and stare
As though they care.

Harvey Morgan (10)
Barton Seagrave Primary School

THE DOLPHIN

The dolphin is a friendly creature
It lives in the deep blue sea
The dolphin is big and blue
It's definitely bigger than me

I have stroked a dolphin before
Rubbery was its skin
In all my dreams, I have wished
To be in the water with a dolphin and swim.

Alex Keyworth (10)
Barton Seagrave Primary School

MY ALPHABET RHYME POEM

A   is for apple where the alphabet starts.
B   is for body which has lots of parts.
C   is for car which goes very fast.
D   is for dog which runs straight past.
E   is for elephant which doesn't drink from a cup.
F   is for fight when people get beaten up.
G   is for grapes which taste very nice.
H   is for hate, particularly mice.
I   is for indigo, the colour I like best.
J   is for Jason who beats all the rest.
K   is for kite which flies high in the sky.
L   is for lemon, you might put in a pie.
M   is for maple, which is so, so sweet.
N   is for nosy, 'Please do not peep.'
O   is for orange, I eat a heap.
P   is for penguin who likes the cold.
Q   is for Quentin who isn't very old.
R   is for robber which I don't like.
S   is for Sam whose dad is called Mike.
T   is for trauma, so much pain!
U   is for umbrella to catch the rain.
V   is for violin which is very hard to play.
W is for Wendy whose birthday is in May.
X   is for X-ray for people who break bones.
Y   is for Yvonne who moans and groans.
Z   is for Zack who ends my alphabet rhyme.
      So why don't you sing my alphabet sometime.

Jennifer Smith (11)
Barton Seagrave Primary School

TURNING BACK TIME

One day a girl wished she could learn
How to turn back the time,
She put her thoughts into words,
Then asked, 'Please Sir, does it have to rhyme?'

The teacher raised an eyebrow
And said to her,
'My dear, what have I just said?'
The girl just shrugged her shoulders,
The teacher shook his head.

'You've obviously not been listening,
No, it doesn't have to rhyme.'
The girl nodded her head
And thought about turning back time.

So now she's produced this poem,
Sadly it doesn't rhyme,
It's about a farmer, his seeds a-sowin',
Trying to turn back time.

'Oh, I wish! Oh, I wish!
I had more time!
If only! If only I could turn back the clock,
I'd be the master of time.'

He broke every clock in the house,
In order to turn back time.
He forgot his seeds and did not pick
Them when they were ripe.

So now you have read her poem,
Which sadly did not rhyme,
Just don't turn like that farmer,
Cos you can't be the master of time.

Alexandra Durling (10)
Barton Seagrave Primary School

KIDS RULE

If kids could rule the school,
It would be really cool,
We would be quite tall,
While the teachers would be small.

The teachers would be in assembly
And we would be at Wembley,
We'd make the teachers suffer,
While we got tougher.

We'd still let them play,
But we'd make them stay
Behind at school,
Cos kids rule.

Chloe Boyall (10)
Barton Seagrave Primary School

DOGS!

Fat ones, thin ones
Small ones, big ones
Brown ones, black ones
Dogs of every size

Fluffy ones, scruffy ones
Dirty ones, clean ones
White ones, grey ones
Dogs of every colour

Dotty ones, spotty ones
Each one's different
Good ones, bad ones
Dogs! Dogs! Dogs!

Hannah Smith (10)
Barton Seagrave Primary School

CHANGES

I know a girl with a pretty face,
She had perfect teeth, no need for a brace.
Her eyes were blue, her nose was small,
But she was very, very tall.

She had no freckles, her face was clear,
Like looking at water from the pier.
Her ears were pierced with pink ear studs,
Her hair as soft as a flower in bud.

But then one day, she fancied a change,
She chopped her hair all wonky and strange.
She started to tell nasty lies,
Which upset people and made them cry.

Nobody liked her anymore,
At least nobody was very sure.
She became bottom of the school,
No one was interested, she wasn't cool.

Eventually she got upset,
Because she was no longer teacher's pet.
She had fallen out with all her friends
And that is what happened in the end.

Jordan Bamsey (10)
Barton Seagrave Primary School

THE PRAYING MANTIS

On the prickly spiky tree,
Crouched the praying mantis
Perfectly he pranced out
Quickly on a fly
Munch and crunch went his lunch.

Sebastian Egan
Barton Seagrave Primary School

SCHOOL

School is fun!
School is boring
Because of the teachers!
School is fun!
School is boring
Because of all the bullies!
School is fun!
School is boring
Because you're drowned with homework!
School is fun!
School is boring
Because of the early morning!
School is fun!
School is great
Because otherwise you wouldn't get anywhere at this rate!

Katharine Blatchly (10)
Barton Seagrave Primary School

THE INSIDE OF THINGS

Inside the grass seed is a glorious meadow,
Inside the acorn is a giant oak tree,
Inside the rosebud is a sweet smelling flower, growing slowly,
Inside the ear of corn is a harvest of wheat ready to eat,
Inside the snowflake is a furious snowball fight,
Inside the wind is an angry hurricane hurrying along,
Inside the raindrop is a fast waterfall falling into a lake,
Inside the child is a heart of gold,
Inside the tear is a happy one waiting to be cried,
Inside the smile is a wave of happiness,
Inside the dream is a place where there are no troubles.

Freya Stapleton (10)
Barton Seagrave Primary School

NOT COMING HOME TONIGHT

I'm not going home tonight,
I might just stroll the streets,
I could get on a plane, an American flight,
But for tea we're having my favourite meat!

I know my mum would worry,
But I'm not allowed to watch TV,
My dad would get in a flurry,
Plus my excuse would probably be measly!

I suppose I could go home,
I could play with my hamster,
I could even have a bath with *loads* of foam,
Plus I could have fun on our banisters!

It's cold and dark now
And I want to go home for tea,
I don't like where we live, full of cows,
Plus I'm dying for a wee!

I really, really want to go home now,
But I've lost my key!

Rebecca Clare Duggan (11)
Barton Seagrave Primary School

SOUND POEM

Splat, mud falling onto the ground
Crunch, biting into an apple
Squeal, braking hard in a car
Sizzle, putting bacon in a pan.

Daniel Martin (9)
Barton Seagrave Primary School

TIME

Time is getting up at five,
I hope I can skive,
Brushing my teeth in the bath,
Walking onto the path,
Into the car I dash,
Eating my potato mash.

Analysing at school,
Catching the ball, cool,
Into the classroom quick,
Sat on the seat with the clock, *tick,*
Teacher came in with a long face,
Drawing pictures and lines in a maze.

The bell rang, it is time to go out,
Ringing, quickly dashing about,
Time to go in again,
What a boring game!
Sitting, listening and sleeping,
Waiting for the time to go fast, creeping.

Justin Wan (11)
Barton Seagrave Primary School

SKIPPING

I'm skipping, skipping, skipping around
I'm skipping in the street
I'm skipping, skipping, skipping
Now I've got to eat
I'm skipping, skipping, skipping around
I'm skipping in the street
I'm skipping, skipping, skipping around
I'm tripping over my feet.

Lauren Ashley (10)
Barton Seagrave Primary School

THE WORLD THROUGH A CHILD'S EYES

The world is peaceful and calm,
There is not such a word as harm,
The bright yellow sunshine,
Above the beautiful blue sea.

The sand under my feet,
The music at a smooth beat,
Making sandcastles,
I sit there on my knees.

It's a wonderful place to be, I say,
That is just its way,
Beautiful and calm,
What a *world!*

The world is peaceful and calm,
There is not such a word as harm,
The bright yellow sunshine,
That's my *world!*

Emily Clipston (11)
Barton Seagrave Primary School

THE INSIDE OF THINGS

Inside the grass seed is a field of smooth grass
Inside the acorn is a huge oak tree
Inside the rosebud is a spiky red flower
Inside the ear of corn is a field of wheat
Inside the snowflake is a mountain of snow
Inside the wind is a shivering breeze
Inside the raindrop is a pot of water
Inside the sunbeam is a shine of light
Inside the book is a miracle to behold.

Benjamin Burgess (9)
Barton Seagrave Primary School

THE INSIDE OF THINGS

Inside the snowflake is a snowman
As light as a cloud
Inside the wind is a storm
Full of sadness
Inside the raindrop is a river
That flows into the sea
Inside the sunbeam
Is a paddling pool waiting for us

Inside the speck of dust
Is a cloud of talcum powder
Inside the stone is a fossil
As dark as night
Inside the brick is a house
With a million bricks
Inside the house is a mansion
As big as Buckingham Palace

Inside the book
Is a library full of adventurous stories
Inside the telephone
Is the unknown message
Inside the computer
Is a store of knowledge
Inside the CD
Is The Ketchup Song to make me dance

Inside the child
Is a heart that will ever last
Inside the tear
Is a past and future
Inside the smile
Is a story of happiness
Inside the dream
Is a wish waiting to happen.

Charlotte Patch (10)
Barton Seagrave Primary School

10 Things Found In A Headmaster's Pocket

A 1927 detention slip
A school report of Jade Wilson
A bundle of broken red biros
A fold-away bamboo cane
A picture of a fat woman in a green dress
A love letter from a girlfriend signed!
A book entitled '360 ways to lie to kids'
A piece of old mouldy biscuit in a blue tissue
A shopping list with 'XXXL headmaster's suit' on
A mug entitled 'Best headmaster in the world!'

Lauren Peploe (10)
Barton Seagrave Primary School

The Inside Of Things

Inside the rosebud is a lovely smell
That never ends

Inside the snowflake is a snowstorm
Blowing against the wind

Inside the speck of dust is a piece of dirt
Made from me and you

Inside the computer is a chip
As powerful as sunlight can be.

Aaron Batten (10)
Barton Seagrave Primary School

THE INSIDE OF THINGS

Inside the book is a fairy tale
Waiting to be freed
Inside the telephone is a voice
Of a mysterious man on the other end
Inside the computer is an e-mail
From a friend
Inside the CD is raging music
That never ends
Inside the child is a heart beating hard
Inside a tear is a raindrop of sadness
Waiting to be forgiven
Inside a smile is a child of happiness
Inside a dream is a nightmare of horror!

Richard Shaw (9)
Barton Seagrave Primary School

TEN THINGS FOUND IN A WIZARD'S POCKET

An invisible cloak
A pack away cauldron
A foldaway broomstick
A shiny golden wand
An enchanted teapot
'Worried Wizards' stress tablets
A packet of 'Everlasting Dead Gerbils'
A pair of big glasses
A spell book entitled 'Make Your Own Fake Hair'
A pair of magic underpants.

Year Five Class Poem
Barton Seagrave Primary School

TEN THINGS FOUND IN A WITCH'S POCKET

A flying monkey with a hat
A Hoover as a broomstick
A smelly goat with a lead
A jar of out of date eyeballs
A book on how to be a good witch
A white owl with a yellow beak
A flying ticket with mud on
A black spellbook of how to uncharm dragons
A shaped wand with sparks coming out of it
A picture of a wizard with a gold frame and hearts on.

Daniel Ginns (9)
Barton Seagrave Primary School

HULLABALOO

H   aughty howling,
U   nsurprised ukulele,
L   aughing lunatic,
L   aconic linguist,
A   djutant alligators,
B   oasting badgers,
A   dvising armadillos,
L   ively lamas,
O   bservant octopuses,
O   verjoyed orang-utans.

Rosie Clark (9)
Beachborough School

AUTUMN POEM

A   pple picking
U   ndergrowth protecting animals
T   ypical blue tits sing in trees, waiting for winter
U   nderground sets of stripy badgers
M   agical colours of dancing leaves
N   aughty squirrels stealing nuts

C   rispy crunching coloured leaves
E   xcited animals scurry about
L   ovely butterflies flutter by
E   nergetic field mice carry corn
B   ees buzzing busily around
R   abbits running, tails bobbing
A   mazing colours autumn brings
T   ortoises slumber in straw-filled boxes
I   ndigo skies full of wild geese
O   wl is looking for mice
N   uts and fruit are growing fast.

Edward Whidborne (10)
Beachborough School

THE BALLET AUDITION

All on our own in that cold draughty hall,
Doesn't bear the thought at all.
My friends are shaking and I have the shivers,
As I sign my paper, my hand gives some quivers.
We're in the hall now dancing away,
Our hearts are pumping fast today.
At last we're out of that dreaded space,
We're out in the open, a wonderful place.

Alex Holburt (10)
Beachborough School

THE LAND OF WIBBELY WONG
(Thanks to Spike Milligan for inspiration)

The land of Wibbely Wong
Where the days are thirty years long
You can sit on your head
Wake up when you're dead
And still be dragged along

In the land of Wibbely Wong
The people aren't very strong
They never lift weights
Or hang out with their mates
And faint at a very loud song

In the land of Wombely Weed
People keep their dogs on a lead
But if it gets free
They will climb up a tree
At a very remarkable speed

In the land of Wumbely Wang
The people live in a gang
They aren't very nice
But if they see mice
They blow up with a very loud bang

In the land of Wimberley Woo
All children are kept in a zoo
They are locked in cages
For ages and ages
What a sensible thing to do!

Peter Fitzsimons (11)
Beachborough School

FOOTBALL CRAZY

F   ast and furious is this game
O   ff goes a player after a reckless shame
O   n comes a substitute after an injured play
T   he ambulance comes to take him away
B   all's been awarded after a penalty kick
A   great big roar after a goal from Mick
L   ying in shame are losing opponents
L   ooking back at the final moments

C   oming first means they win the cup
R   ight at the time they can now look up
A   crobatics is how they celebrate
Z   ubervic the manager congratulates his coaching mate
Y   ou know now it's *football crazy.*

Jamie Patmore (10)
Beachborough School

SCORPIONS

S   cary and spooky as they scamper along,
C   reepy and clever as they catch their prey,
O   bviously occupied with cunning plans,
R   unning rascals who wrap around,
P   lenty of these pests live in North Africa,
I   ndolently eating the insect they've stung,
O   bservantly operating in the desert,
N   ightly, nippy and very naughty,
S   neakily, slithering softly southwards.

Alex Williams (10)
Beachborough School

IN THE SHED

Behind a handy tool,
Leans a terrible ghoul.

Under a bright red wagon,
Hides a fearsome dragon.

Beside a tin can,
Stands a bogeyman.

Near the dog's bones,
The skeleton groans.

By the fencepost,
Lies a trembling ghost.

Beneath the wood pyre,
Lurks a grinning vampire.

Strange shadows in the moonlight,
Gives old Grandad a fright!

Toby Cope (11)
Beachborough School

FEELINGS

F   eelings are things to treasure for life.
E   very time they grow and grow,
E   xtremely strange they never end.
L   ove, hate, happiness, woe.
I   nside everyone there is a spark,
N   othing can retrace this mark.
G   lowing, shining in your soul,
S   itting, smiling, waiting there,
    Feelings should be things to share.

Charlotte Whiteley (10)
Beachborough School

THE HUNT

I hear the sound of the horn
Echoing through the cold night air
I start to run
Deadly dogs bark
I leave the chicken stolen from the hen house
My heart pounds
As I run through the long wet grass
Sounds get closer
Teeth flash in the moonlight
Two dogs appear
Eyes sparkling wildly
Waiting for a moment to pounce
I take flight again
Howls follow my footsteps
Panting fills the air
Closer and closer
Faster and faster
My blood runs cold
Sweat runs from my fur
Legs feel heavy
Dogs gaining
Branches part
Twigs snap
Familiar smells, familiar sounds
Home in sight
One last spurt, angry roars
Safety!

Harry Adams (10)
Beachborough School

DAYDREAM READING

Sitting at my desk,
Wondering what to do,
Sir comes up and says,
'Get working you!'

Suddenly in a daydream,
I find myself in a book,
I decide to turn the page
And go and have a look.

Just as I found Alice,
In her wonderland,
We were under chase
By the Queen of Hearts' band!

Back into a daydream,
I find myself in a book,
I decide to turn the page
And go and have a look.

Flying on my broomstick,
At a Hogwarts Quidditch match,
Hovering and looking,
For the Snitch I'm trying to catch.

Back into a daydream,
I find myself in a book,
I decide to turn the page
And go and have a look.

Then I went to Charlie,
In the chocolate factory,
Eating lots and lots of sweets,
For instance *hair toffee*.

But then Sir came up to see
And said, 'Done any work for me?'

James Bevington (10)
Beachborough School

MIDNIGHT

When midnight struck,
Mice were scuttling,
Owls hooting,
Bats flapping,
Dogs howling,
Branches rustling,
Hedgehogs scurrying,
Deer barking,
Badgers rolling,
Foxes running,
Rabbits thumping,
Otters splashing,
Pigeons cooing,
Robins hiding,
The moon shines down,
Silence falls,
The forest is asleep.

Katie Wilson (10)
Beachborough School

HULLABALOO

H   ilarious hissing
U   nder-exposed underpants
L   ethal leopard
L   aughing litterbug
A   bominable alligator
B   ouncing belly laugh
A   ggravating anteater
L   udicrous laughter
O   pen-hearted otter
O   ver-eager ostrich.

Henry Spencer (9)
Beachborough School

MOUNTAINS

Mountains,
Peacefully quiet,
Mountain tops pointing freely,
Beautiful calm trees brushing,
Eye-catching,
Bigfoot,
Dangerous offending,
Feet like boulders,
Scared of the sight,
Unknown.

Joshua Tokley (9)
Braunston CE Primary School

MY TEACHER IS CRAZY

My teacher is crazy,
She really is mad
And she goes crazy,
When people are bad.

She dances around the classroom,
When everyone is pleasant,
But when she stops, she goes to the floor
And starts running after a pheasant.

The class want her to go
And so does every teacher,
They want her to go to see a doctor
And definitely not become a preacher.

Sam Penhall (10)
Braunston CE Primary School

MOUNTAINS

Mountains
Capacious peaks
Eagle, soaring elegantly
Deserted, marvellous landscape
Forever peaceful
Abominable snowman
Bloodthirsty creature
Threat to mankind
Razor-sharp flint for grinding
Beast.

Robbie Bunn (9)
Braunston CE Primary School

MOUNTAINS

Rocks
Raging dragon
Boulders rattling rapidly
Enraged boulders thundering around
Beast

Mountain
Huge, massive
Relaxing, sleeping eyes
All is peaceful now
Silent.

Edward Gilbert (10)
Braunston CE Primary School

WAR TIMES!

Bang! Boom!
People hearing noise
All around when hiding
In their Anderson shelters

Bang! Boom!
People scared to death
In the war

Bang! Boom!
Children missing
Their mothers and fathers

Bang! Boom!
Every second of the day
This happens 24 hours a day

Bang! Boom!
People shouting
'We hate Hitler!
We hate Hitler!
We hate Hitler!'

Jordan Childs (11)
Braunston CE Primary School

MOUNTAINS

Waterfall
Rippling gently
Majestic, magical, flowing
Calm, incredible, cascading water
Spectacular.

Bethany Whitlow (9)
Braunston CE Primary School

SHELTERING

I hear it first
The loud wailing siren
I can't see
Everything is dark

Next, I hear the drone
Of engines
Softly at first
Then louder, louder still

Suddenly the sky lights up
Following an enormous bang
The engine noise is fading
After a while I hear voices

People are looking, screaming
To see the damage
To look for loved ones
I wish the war would end.

I'm frightened.

Thomas Hill (10)
Braunston CE Primary School

SNOW

Snow
White blanket
Glistening all day
In the shimmering sun
Magical.

Laura Cooper (10)
Braunston CE Primary School

MOUNTAIN

Mountain
Magically spacious
Rippling waterfalls cascading
Magnificently calm and still
Delightful

Yeti
Shaggy-haired, scruffy
Stomping carelessly around
Lonesomely drooping in fog
Spooky.

Sarah Iland (9)
Braunston CE Primary School

MOUNTAIN

Mountain
Vigorously scented
Whistling peacefully, magically
Moving gently with ease
Breathtaking

Bigfoot
Terrific, ghostly
Stampeding over water
Being sighted in mountains
Mysteriously.

Emma Gibson (10)
Braunston CE Primary School

MOUNTAINS

Mountain
Majestic, huge
Butterflies fluttering lightly
Calm, relaxed, sleepy, peaceful
Magnificent

Goat
Slow, energetic
Fur blows gently
Peacefully walking up solitarily
Lonely.

Katrina Edwards (10)
Braunston CE Primary School

MOUNTAINS

Waterfall
Rippling waves
Tumbling spring water
Misty fluent hiking river
Stunning!

Mountain leopard
Frolicking, rolling
Laying, roaring, groaning
With calm beastly instinct
Harmless beast!

Justin Boneham (10)
Braunston CE Primary School

RACING POEM

The race has started
Schumacher's leading
Coulthard's second
Trulli's crashed
Barrichello's in the pits
Montoya's third
Ralf's gone flying
Button's retired
Frentzen's fourth
Villeneuve's wheels came off
Sato's nose came off
The race ended.

Jordan Hearn (10)
Braunston CE Primary School

WATERFALL

Waterfall
Relaxing peacefully
Water flowing gently
Resting in the breeze
Peace

Mountain
Studying valleys
Hard rocks tumbling
With mountain goats watching
Silence.

Jonathan Westall (9)
Braunston CE Primary School

FRANCE GOVERNMENT

F   rance
R   evolution
A   ngry
N   erving
C   ountry
E   vent

G   overned
O   ver
V   ery
E   nviously
R   uthlessly
N   ever-ending
M   urder
E   very
N   ight
T   error.

William Haynes (11)
Braunston CE Primary School

MOUNTAIN

Mountain
High above
Studying all below
Peaceful enough to sleep
Giant.

Benjamin Lord (9)
Braunston CE Primary School

GOLDEN EAGLE

Golden eagle
Egg protector
Swiftly
Swooping around
Magnificent, beautiful
Golden bird
Worthy looking.

Marcus Banks (10)
Braunston CE Primary School

LEAVE ME ALONE CAT

He's strong but wrong
He takes my food
I go off in a mood
I am old and loyal
He's young and smells like oil
He needs more training
He doesn't like it raining

He attacks my tail
Like I'm a giant whale
He's gone for a day
I've got to say, hooray
I've just had enough
He's too naughty and rough
I'm an old cat, so let's leave it at that.

Oliver Lloyd-Wright (10)
Braunston CE Primary School

MY CAT, TIDDLES

Tiddles, my cat
Is very, very fat,
He is *so* big,
He can't even dig.

All he does is eat and snore
And eat and gnaw,
All he does is eat and sleep,
So I can't sleep a peep.

Tiddles, my cat
Is very, very fat,
He eats a lot of food as such,
But I love him so, so much!

Kelly Ford (10)
Braunston CE Primary School

MY DOG, BLUE

My dog is called Blue,
He does sneeze but he doesn't say *atishoo,*
He barks when I run
And barks when he's having fun.

My dog, Blue
Runs round and round
Trying to catch his tail,
He eats his food so quick,
He nearly makes himself sick.

Tobias Underwood (10)
Braunston CE Primary School

KISMET

Kismet is our little dog
Black and white and friendly too
About three years old and fond of play
When we come home from school each day
She likes to dance and fight
We go for walks and rabbits run
Our little dog has lots of fun

Kismet likes to chew on bones
You never hear her really moan
She has eyes that are brown
You never ever see her frown
She is the most wonderful thing
That you have ever seen
But I have to say goodbye.

Poppy Anne Simmons (10)
Braunston CE Primary School

FAIR

I like to go to the fair,
I like to see what's there,
I like to go on the big wheel
And listen to everyone squeal,
I like to go to the fair.

Shane Davis (10)
Braunston CE Primary School

MY CATS

My cat is different to other cats,
She doesn't like to chase,
She won't run after any rats,
She won't even race.

My other cat, she likes to scratch,
Anything that's in sight,
It makes my dad go as red as a match,
Which happens every night.

Last there's my favourite which I adore,
She's very, very black
And all she really likes to do is eat and snore
And sleep in a sack.

Rebecca Cox (11)
Braunston CE Primary School

WAR

W ide open trenches
    Rotten body stenches
    The fist clenches
    Am I going to die?

A dolf Hitler is cruel
    Many died under his rule
    Oh the silly fool
    He thinks he's going to win

R eeling in pain
    Trying to escape their chain
    This is all inhumane
    That's World War II.

Sarah Green (10)
Braunston CE Primary School

MISSING MY MUM

I am missing my mum because she is far away,
I had to leave, to leave her the other day,
I miss the way she kissed me goodnight,
I miss the way she tucked me in tight.

I am missing my mum because she is far away,
I really want to see her more every day,
I miss the way she held my hand,
I miss the way she combed my hair.

I am missing my mum because she is far away,
I had to say bye on the train,
I miss the sweet smell of her perfume,
I miss the way she held me tight.

I am missing my mum because she is far away,
I can only see her in my head,
I miss the way we snuggled up tight,
I miss the way we talked and talked.

I am missing my mum because she is so far away,
I really want to hear her soft voice,
I miss the way she used to read to me,
I miss the way she tickled me,
I am missing my mum because she is far away,
I had to leave her the other day.

Alexandria Natasha Hart (11)
Braunston CE Primary School

WHEN THE SNOW FALLS

When the snow falls
It's nice and soft

When the snow falls
I like to throw snowballs

When the snow falls
Everyone has fun

When the snow falls
People make snowmen

When the snow falls
The ground is crunchy

When the snow falls
It's Christmas.

Joshua Sullivan (8)
Braunston CE Primary School

SNOW-WHITE

The polar bear's fur, white as snow,
The polar bear's teeth, as sharp as the tip of an iceberg,
The polar bear's eyes, as shiny as the icy ocean.

The polar bear's feet, as fast as an avalanche,
The polar bear's nose, as sensitive as icicles,
The polar bear's asleep among the snug cave.

Chanelle Aspinwall (10)
Braunston CE Primary School

HORROR CLASSES AT BRAUNSTON SCHOOL

The worst class could be reception,
Full of untruths and deception,
If you think they're sweet,
Just look at the heat,
The worst class might be reception.

But maybe it might be Class 1,
They are but incredibly strong,
So if you think you've seen
A class half as mean,
You've certainly been to Class 1.

The worst class might be Class 2,
Their classroom looks a bit like a loo,
There's paper here and there,
So I think it's fair,
The worst class might be Class 2.

Then again it might be Year 3,
They're doing Hinduism you see,
They're painting red spots
All over their tops,
The worst year could be Year 3.

The worst class could be Year 4,
They've smashed their purple class door,
It might be Year 5,
They're certainly alive,
Is the worst class Year 4 or Year 5?

The worst class is definitely Year 6,
They went on a residential school trip,
They put lice in the pants
Of endangered elephants,
The worst class is *definitely* Year 6!

Rebecca Broadley (10)
Braunston CE Primary School

DOLPHINS

Dolphins are smooth
Dolphins eat fish
Dolphins do tricks
And jump high in the sky

Dolphins are cute
Dolphins are clever
Wherever they are
They don't mind the weather

Oh, how I wish
I had a good friend
Like a dolphin.

Danielle Childs (11)
Braunston CE Primary School

FORCES

Forces keep you on the ground,
Forces push you up,
Forces make friction.

Forces have to be fat,
Forces can be slim,
Forces are brilliant in the middle.

Forces help everyone,
Forces go against you,
Forces hurt people.

Kallum John Bell (10)
Braunston CE Primary School

FRIENDS

They always tell you to do your best
Friends can be there when you get in a mess
They're always there when you need them around
When they come over, they always make a sound

One of them wears glasses
When they come over, they eat masses and masses
One of them is called Hatty
She's the one that's really chatty

You dream about them in your sleep
Friends are always there to keep
But most of all the bottom line
Don't forget your friends in time.

Marisa Harrison (10)
Braunston CE Primary School

MY DOG

My dog secretly tries to eat the table and chairs
And he chews up all my toys
So he's not allowed upstairs

When my mum is ironing out clothes and underwear
The dog goes to sleep in the basket
But my mum doesn't really care.

Samantha Green (10)
Braunston CE Primary School

WHEN THE SNOW FALLS

When the snow falls
I make a snowman

When the snow falls
I go sledging in the snow

When the snow falls
The water freezes up

When the snow falls
I go out to play

When the snow falls
I play snowball fights

When the snow falls
I go for a walk

When the snow falls
It gets cold.

Hannah Miller (9)
Braunston CE Primary School

SHIVERS

Snow is cold, as cold as ice
Snow is soft, as soft as a teddy bear
Snow is light, as light as a feather
Snow is white, as white as a white blanket
And me, I just like to lay in it.

Kieran Spencer (9)
Braunston CE Primary School

SNOW!

I'm sitting in the classroom nice and quietly
When someone shouts, 'Snow, snow!'
We all peer through the window
When suddenly the play time bell rings
Coats, hats, scarves and gloves are quickly put on

We all run outside like a bullet flying through the air
I looked up, it was like a thousand flies floating around me
But it wasn't, it was snow.

Tenisha Mistry (8)
Braunston CE Primary School

ON SNOWY NIGHTS

On snowy nights people cuddle up tight
By the fire they clutch hands
And think about all the people on warm lands
Oh, what a beautiful sight

On snowy nights people go carol singing
Children draw pictures of snow
Santa's coming, ho ho ho!
The kid brought a snowball to fling.

Jessica Bennett (9)
Braunston CE Primary School

IT'S SNOWING

It's snowing
Crunch, munch
It's snowing
Munch, crunch
It's snowed the whole day long

The rooftop's white
And the window's ice
Fluttery, muttering
With the snow's song.

Joshua Rowe (8)
Braunston CE Primary School

MAGICAL SNOW

Crinch, crunch
It's snowing
Cripple, crapple
It's snowing
It's been snowing
All day
Flitter, flutter
Floaty flakes
Dancing to the ground
Slishy, slushy,
Squelch, squelch
It's melting
Yucky, slushy
It's disappeared
Out of sight.

Margaret Coleman (9)
Braunston CE Primary School

SNOW, SNOW, SNOW

Look at all the children in the snow,
People skating very, very low,
Children playing all day long,
Adults singing Christmas songs,
That's snow, snow
Guess what?
Snow!

Anika Madan (9)
Braunston CE Primary School

WHEN THE SNOW FALLS

When the snow falls feet squeak
When the snow falls people squeak
When the snow falls animals hide
When the snow falls cars go eek
When the snow falls people slip.

Thomas Findlay (9)
Braunston CE Primary School

FLITTERY, FLUTTERY SNOW

Flittery, fluttery, falling snow
Swirling around and around you go
Floating gently to the ground
Coming down without a sound
Falling down flake by flake
Looking as beautiful as a cake.

Helen Ansell (9)
Braunston CE Primary School

SNOW

Snow is cold, freezing too
Dish, dash

Snow is a big white blanket
Flish, flosh

Water is inside it
Dash, dosh

Snow is the colour white
Hawk, hack

What I think that would be nice
Crunch, crack

If there was a great big sack!
Lock, lack.

Amy Blundell (9)
Braunston CE Primary School

DANCING SNOW

The snow dances day and night
Looping and swooping, so lovely and bright
Straining to see the lovely sight
But it's still horrid because it packs a fight
Dancing snow, dancing snow
I love the snow
Ho ho ho!

Alex Curtis (9)
Braunston CE Primary School

WHEN THE SNOW FALLS

When the snow falls
There's no warmth about

When the snow falls
Animals hibernate, children shout

When the snow falls
Teachers do work, children play

When the snow falls
It's cold and adults say we can't play

When the snow falls
Creatures die, birds fly high

When the snow falls
My dad makes a pie.

Shaun Tippett (8)
Braunston CE Primary School

I'M WALKING IN THE SNOW

I'm walking in the snow
It's falling, falling, you'll never hear a bird crowing

I'm walking in the snow
It's wet, wet, wet, no good for throwing

I'm walking . . . but the snow has gone.

Briony Martin (8)
Braunston CE Primary School

WHEN THE SNOW FALLS

When the snow falls
People sledge all day

When the snow falls
People shout, 'Look out!'

When the snow falls
People throw snowballs

When the snow falls
People make snowmen

And I do too.

Holly Webb (9)
Braunston CE Primary School

I'M WALKING SLOWLY THROUGH THE SNOW

I'm walking slowly through the snow
While snowflakes drift past me

I'm walking slowly through the snow
While the branches creak on the chestnut tree

I'm walking slowly through the snow
Crinch, crunch, crinch, crunch, the sound of my shoes

I'm walking slowly through the snow
There's a beautiful snowman, I wonder whose?

Sally Hall (8)
Braunston CE Primary School

WHEN THE SNOW FALLS

When the snow falls
On the rooftops
When the snow falls
It flutters and hops
When the snow falls
It pops in your hand
When the snow falls
It covers the land
When the snow falls
It is sparkly and white
When the snow falls
You can have a snow fight.

Matthew Haynes (8)
Braunston CE Primary School

WHEN THE SNOW FALLS

When the snow falls, it's crunchy and cold
When the snow falls, I play snowballs
When the snow falls, it's bitter and bright
When the snow falls, I love the sights
When the snow falls, I dream of knights
When the snow falls, the blazing fire is so lovely and bright
When the snow falls, oh when the snow falls, it's lovely and bright.

Joseph Crooks (9)
Braunston CE Primary School

WHEN THE SNOW FALLS

When the snow falls
People dance, stick their tongue out

When the snow falls
White snow fairies twirl about

When the snow falls
It's everlasting and priceless

When the snow falls
It's a bunch of brightness

When the snow falls
People rush out their houses to play

When the snow falls
People go in for the night and wait for the next day

When the snow falls
People sledge all day long

When the snow falls
Children sing a special song

When the snow falls
Wrap up warm, it's cold

When the snow falls
It's so young, it's almost old.

Amy Roberts (9)
Braunston CE Primary School

Snow, Snow, Snow

Snow is thick, it's up to my knee,
Snow is white, as white as can be,
Snow is *crunch, crunch, crunch*,
Snow tastes icy, *munch, munch, munch*,
Snow is soft as a soft teddy bear,
Snow is cool and it's everywhere.

Nancy Leach (9)
Braunston CE Primary School

My Favourite . . .

Finger nipper,
Water tipper.

Polo snatcher,
Apple catcher.

Carrot eater,
Race beater.

Little bucker,
Stable mucker.

Dirt maker,
Food taker.

My one and only,
Little . . .

Pony.

Charlotte Goetz (10)
Croughton All Saints Primary School

THE WORST DAY OF MY LIFE

Bike nicker,
Tool picker.

Lock breaker,
Crime maker.

Police bringer,
Alarm ringer.

Radio snatcher,
Jewellery catcher.

In your world you are the chief,
But in my world you are a . . .

Thief.

Lauren Jane Jacob (9)
Croughton All Saints Primary School

THE LAND OF MOUNTAIN ICE

All the different colours are blending into each other
Cream, delicious whites that look like blobs of snow
Strawberry swirl, pinks of flowers and chocolate browns of the earth
The lovely sticky milky mess in puddles all around
They're melting every second, dripping down the mountain of ice
It's like it's snowing, wet and slippery
All of the colours cascading over like a waterfall down the mountain
Then suddenly the sun comes out and it gets hotter and hotter
And the mountain melts to the ground.

Rachael Hayes (10)
Croughton All Saints Primary School

MY BEST FRIEND

A tail flicker,
A finger nipper.

A messy eater,
A bar chewer.

A strong kicker,
A food nicker.

A carrot chewer,
An apple taker.

A polo snatcher,
A water licker.

A good winner,
A fast runner.

My best friend is a horse.

Megan Forbes (9)
Croughton All Saints Primary School

MY FAVOURITE PET IS A ...

Bubble blower,
Graceful swimmer,
Gill breather,
Aquarium dweller,
Sunday's dish,
I'm a . . .

Fish.

Dale Hodgins (10)
Croughton All Saints Primary School

THE LAND OF SWEETS

The land of sweets is the place to be,
So wobble on down to the candyfloss tree.
I think you'll agree, it's the best in the land,
With peppermint rain and choco-pops snow.
Try custard, yum, you'll like it I know,
You could listen to the lollipop band.
On the Milky Way hill it sounds grand,
Watch the candyfloss clouds float by,
Come to the land of sweets and *try, try, try!*

Peter Andrew (10)
Croughton All Saints Primary School

BUBBLEGUM

Bubblegum, bubblegum,
Soft, pink and chewy bubblegum,
Some think it's boring, I think it's fun,
Blowing bubbles with my gum!

See how big the bubble gets,
Before it pops and leaves a mess!
'You're grounded!' said Mum,
'What a mess!'
When she saw the stain my bubblegum left.
Now I'm banned from bubblegum,
Pink, soft, beloved bubblegum.

Samantha Stewart (11)
Daventry Grange Junior School

TEN THINGS UNDER MY SISTER'S BED

What is under my sister's bed is . . .

A packet of candy cigarettes,
Pictures of relatives
And snapshots of friends
Chewing gum and old sweet wrappers,
Loads of money hidden from me,
Old tapes waiting to be played,
Toys from childhood days,
Stacks of books that have never been read,
Old records from 1870
And posters of Will Young.

Casey Cooper (11)
Daventry Grange Junior School

JUNGLE

In the jungle . . .

J   aguars with giant jaws
U   nusual creatures unknown to man
N   oisy creatures in the trees
G   iant gorillas, kings of trees
L   ions lying lazily on the ground
E   xtraordinary elephants drinking in the lake.

Josephine Thompson (10)
Daventry Grange Junior School

TEN THINGS FOUND IN A WIZARD'S POCKET!

The same sunny summer
An ant-eating antelope
A blue baboon bouncing bonkers
A cat crouching on a chair
A dozing donkey demolishing a dandelion
An electrifying eel enjoying an egg
A flamingo flying fast in freezing air
A gambling goat getting gammon
A hairy hare hiding in a hat
A wolf snoring.

Lucy Shepherd (11)
Daventry Grange Junior School

TEN THINGS FOUND IN A WITCH'S WAND

A dark black night
All the words you couldn't spell
A broomstick which couldn't fly
A cloak covered with stars and moons
A spell to turn you blue
A crystal ball predicting your dreams
A letter from the spellbook shop
A black cat splashing in cream
A spell to tell your future
A dream black cat.

Katrina Duncan (10)
Daventry Grange Junior School

BEST PLACES

A beach,
Golden sands and a bright blue sea,
Just ready for me to dive in.

A pool,
Nice and cool,
Where the diving board is and I bomb.

My bedroom,
A big pool table,
My pool stick ready for me to play with.

Dolphin swimming,
I jump on its back,
It swims deep down and pops back up again.

Nathan Pow (10)
Daventry Grange Junior School

TEN THINGS FOUND UNDER MY BROTHER'S BED

A dented black tin with a huge ship on the lid.
An old love letter from an old flame.
A glass of rancid, curdled milk.
A large plastic lorry from his nursery days.
A piece of chewing gum stuck to a shoe.
A Game Boy Advance all shiny and new.
A wallet full of pounds and pence.
A bucket full of plastic cars.
A bag of sweets and a box of chocs.
A snoring cat and a barking dog.

Luke Ireland (10)
Daventry Grange Junior School

TEN THINGS FOUND IN A WITCH'S POCKET

A dark knight,
Some chocolate that you couldn't eat,
A bowl of soup overflowing,
A large snake eating her pocket,
A wound glowing in the dark,
A packet of sweets melting away,
A little mouse crying for his mum,
A pair of glasses, broken,
A watch ticking away,
A bit of chalk messing and breaking into dust.

Shane Parry (11)
Daventry Grange Junior School

SOMEWHERE, UNDERGROUND IN A TREE

Somewhere,
Underground in a tree,
You will find
And of course will see,
A giant, big bowling ball,
About to crash into a wall,
A small ball of wool,
Horribly, grey and dull.

Somewhere,
Underground in a tree,
You will find
And of course will see,
The smallest man in the land,
With a giant fan in his hand
And last but not least, a heap of yeast,
100 grams or at least.

Jade Sutton (11)
Daventry Grange Junior School

HULLABALOO!

I'll tell you a little tale,
That is completely true,
When I came home from school one day,
My house was full with animals from the zoo,
In the kitchen there were a couple of monkeys,
They were sat there making a brew,
I went to the shed where a snake lay
And he was playing around with glue,
I was really, really puzzled,
Whatever should I do?
Then to my surprise before my eyes,
Went bouncing a kangaroo,
Round and round the living room,
A pelican and flamingo flew
And when I went upstairs to the bathroom,
There was a crocodile in the loo!
But my bedroom was completely empty,
Soon the rest of the house was too,
They all went dancing round the garden,
That's what I call *hullabaloo!*

Hayley Irons (10)
Daventry Grange Junior School

ANGER POEM

Anger feels like broken glass,
Anger sounds like a banshee screaming,
Anger looks like a winded rhinoceros,
Anger smells like burnt toast,
Anger tastes like a year-old pizza.

Kyle Langlands (10)
Daventry Grange Junior School

TEN THINGS FOUND IN A BEAUTICIAN'S POCKET

A brand new comb that's never been used,
A list of the customers' favourite shoes,
Different colour contacts for their eyes,
Packets of brown and blond hair dyes,
Lipsticks of red, pink and brown,
Addresses of the best clothes shops in town,
A make-up bag full of bits and bobs,
Her house key and her broken door knob,
Eyeliner and mascara just for fun
And packets and packets of chewing gum.

Eryn Pinfold (10)
Daventry Grange Junior School

TEN THINGS FOUND IN THE OCEAN

A big killer shark with a massive fin
A spread-out octopus with a great big grin
A big green turtle flapping his flippers
There's a girl swimming in her slippers
A lot of seaweed just swaying there
The lazy fish just float and stare
The sea horses racing like athletes
Starfish crawling in fleets
The dolphins jumping up and down
And most of all the sea is seaweed, big and brown.

Ashleigh Gallacher (11)
Daventry Grange Junior School

TEN THINGS FOUND IN A KANGAROO'S POUCH

A crystal squashed by fluff and wool,
An elephant's baby just having fun,
A rose torn from top to bottom,
A little joey fast asleep,
A small puppy chasing its tail,
A naughty parrot nibbling his way out,
A little girl with natural curls,
My old nan, with diamonds and pearls,
A flower growing from its roots,
A creepy spider making a web.

Megan Guest (11)
Daventry Grange Junior School

TEN THINGS FOUND IN A GLOOMY ATTIC

A creaky floor that made a sound,
A big creepy skeleton, lost and found,
A box of photographs ripped and torn,
Some coins and notes, from lands afar,
A creepy-crawly, climbing the wall,
An old fur coat that touched the floor,
A video from long ago,
In the corner a mouse sleeps,
An old broken window cracked by a stone,
A light smashed on the floor.

Lauren Farmer (10)
Daventry Grange Junior School

TEN THINGS FOUND IN A HUMAN BODY

A dull place,
Where nobody goes,
Where green things lurk
And speed out of your nose,
A stomach where all your food falls,
When you are hungry,
It rumbles and calls,
The brain is pink,
When you are stuck,
It makes you think,
Calculating an answer in a heartbeat.

Daniel Brownson (10)
Daventry Grange Junior School

TEN THINGS FOUND IN A WIZARD'S POCKET

A wizard's wand
Stars and glass that would never break
Frogs' legs and cats' eyes ready for boiling
Spearmints you could suck forever
A crystal ball, with a lot to tell
An African elephant washing in the midday sun
An old spellbook tattered and torn
And a baby who has just been born
A furry rabbit at the bottom
And a little ball made out of cotton.

Alexander James Griffin (11)
Daventry Grange Junior School

QUEENY, CAN YOU COOK?

Queeny was in her throne, she was reading a book
When I tapped on her shoulder to see if she could cook
'Queeny, can you cook? Can you cook? Can you, Queeny?'
And she looked up and said to me
'Dear, I'm the best cooking queen this world's seen,
I'm a knife, fork, spoon, sieve, cook-cook queen.'

And she rose from her throne in the middle of the room
And she started to cook with her veggies and fruit
And she cooked past my dad and she cooked past my mother
She cooked past me and my little brother
I could hear her voice saying, 'Listen dear,
Listen to the cooking of the cook-cook queen
I'm the best cooking queen this world's seen
I'm a knife, fork, spoon, sieve
Bowl, plate, ice cream,
Cooking, cooking
Cook-cook queen.'

Abbi Griffiths (10)
Daventry Grange Junior School

ANGER

Anger smells like a cave full of bats
Anger looks like blood-red flames of a burning fire
Anger sounds like thunder clashing with a big bang of thunder
Anger feels like you're on fire
Anger tastes like a dead fish in your mouth.

Allan Webster (9)
Daventry Grange Junior School

JOY

Joy smells like the first flower in spring
Joy looks like the golden sun rising in a summer morning
Joy sounds like the first breath of a newborn child
Joy feels like a butterfly touching your arm
Joy tastes like vanilla ice cream with extra chocolate sauce.

Abbie Weaving (10)
Daventry Grange Junior School

ANGER

Anger feels like a devil scratching at your heart
Anger looks like a red puffed-up face
Anger smells like wood burning in the midnight fire
Anger sounds like rubbish crashing in the bin
Anger tastes like rotten eggs
Anger fills your head with fire.

Ryan Midson (10)
Daventry Grange Junior School

ANGER

Anger smells like smoke drifting on the breeze
Anger looks like red lava from a volcano
Anger feels like hot fire that can kill
Anger sounds like a volcano erupting
Anger lasts like bitter soapsuds in your mouth.

Jamie Bryson (9)
Daventry Grange Junior School

HAPPINESS

Happiness smells like
A bunch of fresh roses

Happiness looks like
A fire blazing on a cold winter's night

Happiness sounds like
School holidays in a busy park

Happiness feels like
Soft sheepskin on bare skin

Happiness tastes like
A child's first birthday cake.

Sarah Lunt (10)
Daventry Grange Junior School

THE THINGS I FOUND INSIDE A SNAIL'S SHELL

A dolphin leaping up and down
Being as cute as can be
An old haggard man begging in the street
A teacher telling children off
Babies crying in the park
Thunder and lightning on and off
A blue whale making a humongous splash
I found many things inside a snail's shell
Much more than you can dream.

Taylor Wemyss (10)
Daventry Grange Junior School

ANGER

Anger smells like a burnt piece of toast
On a Sunday morning

Anger looks like the Earth
Getting sucked up by the ground

Anger sounds like a big red balloon
Popping in the sky

Anger feels like a red ant
Biting your leg

Anger tastes like a hungry lion.

Emily Holdridge (9)
Daventry Grange Junior School

LONELINESS

Loneliness smells like
A burnt cake that's been left cold
Loneliness looks like
A small child being kept in a rusty cage
Loneliness feels like
A day when your mates leave you
Loneliness sounds like a baby crying
But nobody comes
Loneliness tastes like a sour lemon
That's been eaten by a baby.

Sophie Sear (9)
Daventry Grange Junior School

HIP HOPPY BIRD!

I'm a hip hoppy bird and you'll never catch me nappin',
No matter where I go, you'll always hear me flappin',
I flap to the south and I flap to the east,
I flap to the mice and I flap to the beast,
I flap to the ground and I drive the woodworm nutty,
I flap to my family when I eat a bacon butty,
I flap to the flies and I flap to the fleas,
I flap to the turf and I flap to the trees,
I've flapped since I flew,
I've flew since I flapped,
Flapping, flying, flying, flapping,
Flapping, flapping, flap.

Joanne Grantham (11)
Daventry Grange Junior School

THE SUN

The sun is bright and beautiful
So shiny and yellow
The sun is very hot when you go to the beach
It is as yellow as a lemon

Sun makes children play
Sun makes people wear summery clothes
People like to sunbathe in the sun
I like sun
It's beautiful and bright
You should like it too.

Andrea Denyer (8)
Daventry Grange Junior School

FLOWER POWER

I love flowers
They have so many powers
I think they smell
I called one Mel
Roses are red
I hate flowers that are dead.

Chloe Ingram *(8)*
Daventry Grange Junior School

THE FOOT

This is the foot that hops around
And leans forward and backwards,
It jumps high and low,
This is the foot with scars,
This is the foot that slipped on a banana
And loves wearing slippers.

Sean Morgan *(9)*
Daventry Grange Junior School

LOVE IS IN THE AIR

Love is in the air
I can hear a dare
I can hear it here and there
People hugging
People kissing
People hate missing.

Amy Cory *(8)*
Daventry Grange Junior School

THIS IS THE ARM

This is the arm that bends and twists
This is the arm that throws
But sometimes it burns in the hot sun
This is the arm that carries bags
When I'm out shopping with my mum.

Matthew Burgoyne (10)
Daventry Grange Junior School

THE SNOWMAN

Some children were making a friendly snowman,
He shines in the sun but doesn't shine at night,
Snow is white and cold,
Snowman is round and fat,
He has a carrot for his nose
And that is the end of the snowman.

Shakira Clare (8)
Daventry Grange Junior School

SNOW

S   oft
N   ice
O   h what a lovely day
W   hite.

Sammy Jo (8)
Daventry Grange Junior School

THE SNOW

The snow is white
The snow is cold
You can make snowballs
You can make snowmen
The snow can make you cold
The snow is soft
The ice is slippy
The ice is black
You can make footprints with your feet.

Sam Ashley (9)
Daventry Grange Junior School

TEN THINGS FOUND IN THE WIZARD'S HAT

A dark night
A large bowl of soup
An elephant with two trunks
A magic book flying around
A racoon biting me
A little rat running
A little goldfish swimming in the sea
A globe with mysteries
A cup of tea to drink on a cold night
A little doll for a girl of three.

Kimm Stainforth (10)
Daventry Grange Junior School

WHAT TEACHERS EAT AT LUNCH!

It's anybody's guess
What teachers eat at lunch
So we held a competition
To see if any of us were right

We did a spot of research
Although some of them wouldn't say
But it's probably something funny
As they look pretty strange by day

Our head teacher, quite old-fashioned
He eats a Sunday roast
Our sports teachers eats fruits
And some salad too

That new teacher in the infants
Eats hamburgers with cheese
Our deputy head eats curries
That he bought back from his travels

We asked our secretary what she ate
But she shooed us out of her room
And our teacher said her favourite's
Chocolate and a cup of tea

And mademoiselle who teaches French
Is really very rude
She whispered, 'Alas! Don't tell a soul
But I eat frogs' legs in my classroom!'

Zeshan Hussain (11)
Daventry Grange Junior School

KID C

My name is Kid C and this is my rhyme,
So sit back folk while I rap my mind.
I rap to the beat and I rap to the tune,
I rap to the sun and I rap to the moon,
I rap to the grass, I rap to the trees,
I rap to the birds and I rap to the bees,
I rap to my mother, I rap to my nan,
I rap to my brother and I rap to my gran,
So I've rapped to you
And I've rapped to me,
I've rapped to the whole world,
As you can see!

Cora Dicks (11)
Daventry Grange Junior School

SADNESS

Sadness feels like a diamond trickling down my cheek.
Sadness sounds like a train whistling past you at a hundred
$$\text{miles per hour.}$$
Sadness looks like a leaf falling off a tree at the end of summer.
Sadness smells like an old rotten orange hidden under a leaf.
Sadness tastes like a rotten apple sitting on the bottom
$$\text{of your fruit bowl.}$$

Alex Tack (10)
Daventry Grange Junior School

JOY

Joy smells like a bunch of roses.
Joy looks like happiness, like a newborn baby.
Joy sounds like people laughing hysterically.
Joy tastes like a piece of my tenth birthday cake.
Joy feels like a newborn baby crying for his mother.

Karl Shingler (9)
Daventry Grange Junior School

JOY

Joy looks like a paradise poking up from behind a hill.
Joy smells like the freshness on the first day of spring.
Joy sounds like people having a brilliant time on holiday.
Joy feels like a newborn family member just been born.
Joy tastes like Angel Delight strawberry flavour, with hundreds
                                        and thousands on top.
Joy is a beaver building a new home!

Charlotte Swain (9)
Daventry Grange Junior School

JOY

Joy smells like swimming in a pool of tulips.
Joy looks like a toddler opening a present on their birthday.
Joy sounds like wedding bells ringing.
Joy feels like a butterfly landing on you in the summer.
Joy tastes like swallowing sweet treacle down your throat.

Emma Holmes (9)
Daventry Grange Junior School

ANGER

Anger smells like the burning of a bush,
Anger feels like a big red balloon is bursting,
Anger looks like your face is on fire,
Anger sounds like Mount Etna has just erupted,
Anger tastes like life without chocolate.

Lloyd Liddington (9)
Daventry Grange Junior School

JOY

Joy tastes like a party in full swing.
Joy looks like Mr Beats having a happy day.
Joy feels like ice cream on my tongue.
Joy sounds like the sea on a calm day.
Joy smells like a cake in the oven.

Sam Morgan (9)
Daventry Grange Junior School

ANGER

Anger smells like smoke floating through the air on a winter's day.
Anger looks like a burning fire through my eyes.
Anger sounds like somebody screaming right through my
                                            ear to the eardrum.
Anger feels like you are about to burst open.
Anger tastes like blood running down your throat.
Anger fills your head with all sorts of red, hot-headed things.

Shannon Wilson (9)
Daventry Grange Junior School

ANGER!

Anger smells like a burnt cake that my dad made,
Anger looks like a droopy funeral all in black on a summer's day,
Anger sounds like a miserable wet rainy day,
Anger feels like a bee stinging you on your birthday,
Anger fills your head with red, bloody, devily rage.

Rhia Dawson (9)
Daventry Grange Junior School

SNOW

Snow is soft and slushy
And you can make it bushy
It glitters in your gardens
It gently falls to the ground
Snow is fun to play with
All children love snow
And snow falls quite low.

Miriam Noor (8)
Daventry Grange Junior School

SNOWMAN

S lippy ice is black
N ow snow is falling from the sky
O n that day a snowman standing at the door
W inter came and I built a snowman in the garden
M other was shocked, she saw a snowman standing
A n icicle fell from the sky
N ow the snowman was gone.

Ricky Jones (8)
Daventry Grange Junior School

THE FAIRGROUND RIDE

I'm wrapped up warm for a chilly, chilly ride,
I climb in and belt up and hold on tight.

Slowly we move towards the dark starlit sky
And the breeze blowing gently,
Through my long blonde hair.

Round and round we go,
Faster, faster,
All the colours of the fairground whizz round and round,
As we are spinning through the air.

Laura Dyson (10)
Daventry Grange Junior School

THE SNOWBALL FIGHT

Snowballs flying everywhere
People scream and shout
Run and hide, snowballs are flying about

'Duck' people shout
Oops, one hit my mother
Oops, one hit my brother

The sun came out
People still play
As the snow melts away.

Jack Reesby (8)
Daventry Grange Junior School

THE SNOWMAN

T winkling snow, falling to the ground,
H iding all year round,
E ntering every town.

S now is beautiful, fluffy and white,
N oble snow, you make me want to squeeze you tight,
O h snow you are so wonderful,
W hen you are not here, I am so dull
M ounding you into a snowman
A lthough I like you, I have to visit my nan
N ow the day is through, you will soon melt away.

Snowman!

Megan-Jade Hall (9)
Daventry Grange Junior School

THE SNOWMAN

S now is so delicate and soft
N o snow would be a disaster
O h snow, I love so much
W oe would be upon us if you did not come
M e, I would cry because you did not come
A child would be very sad if you did not come
N oble snow of the sky, I wish you would come every day.

Alexander Lee (8)
Daventry Grange Junior School

SNOW TOWNS

Snow is falling on the town
It hasn't snowed all year round
If you leave me, I will frown
But you're lying silently on the ground

The town is white
Trees are bare with silver
The snow is bright
But I sometimes shiver.

Harry Caulton (8)
Daventry Grange Junior School

SNOW STREET

The snow is white
It comes mostly at night
Snow's a nice sight
In December
It gives me
Things to remember
After a while
The snow starts to disappear
After a while I get cold ears
I can't wait until it snows again.

Shane Sutton (9)
Daventry Grange Junior School

SNOW

This morning I woke up and looked outside
I saw the greatest thing
Little white balls falling from the sky
I jumped out of my bed
I looked around me
I ran outside
To see the excitement that was here
We threw snowballs at each other
The trees were covered in snow
The roofs of the houses were white
The sun comes up to greet us
We play all day
And the sun went down at the end of the day
And then we went to bed.

Georgina Bryers (8)
Daventry Grange Junior School

SNOW

Snow is so white
Snow is so fluffy and soft
Snow is when everyone goes ice-skating
Snowflakes and Jack Frost come in the winter's night
And everyone slips on the black ice.

Adam Creaney (8)
Daventry Grange Junior School

THE SNOW

The snow is falling to the ground
It hasn't snowed all year round
Why, I have not a clue
The town is just as beautiful as you

Some people say you make them cold
Even if I am bold
I will always think you are wonderful
Even if I am told you are not useful.

Bronwen Edwards (9)
Daventry Grange Junior School

THE SNOWMAN

I saw this snowman, I asked if he wanted to come in,
He just stood there,
Then I got him some underwear,
He just stood there,
Then I gave him a biscuit,
He just stood there,
Then I let him watch TV,
He just stood there,
I thought he might want an ice cream,
He just stood there,
I went upstairs, found a book,
I went downstairs and there was nothing there.

James Moore (9)
Daventry Grange Junior School

SNOWFALL

Snow is falling, white and slippy,
Snow fights everywhere,
People making snowmen.
As the sun comes up
Some of it slowly fades away,
Ponds are iced up and cold,
Snow is slushy.
People skiing down the hill
Covered in snow,
The clouds are grey,
Snowflakes are falling again,
And everyone is playing with the snow.

Amy Pow (9)
Daventry Grange Junior School

THE SNOWMAN

S lushy snowman was standing outside,
N ow icicles were falling off the trees,
O n that big white bed the snowman stood,
W inter came and the snow was falling,
M oon came up and the snowman stood there all night,
A snowman stood outside the window and blinked,
N ow the snowman stood on the snow and smiled.

Shannon Craig (8)
Daventry Grange Junior School

SNOWY PARK

Snowy it is at this time of year,
Slushy and slippery all around,
Snowflakes fall on top of the slide,
We all try to hide underneath the snow,
This is my favourite place to skid and slide,
But as it starts to fade away I'm sad,
Snowy park I call this place,
The winter has passed,
It comes to an end,
It will come again and make me happy again.

Corina Staires (8)
Daventry Grange Junior School

CAT POEM

Fast runner
Lovely player
Brilliant climber
Horrible biter
Long sleeper
Great miaower
Beautiful purrer
Nasty scratcher

Cat.

Rebecca Pucci (8)
Daventry Grange Junior School

This Is The Eye

This is the eye
that saw a show
that winked to a friend
that saw a dolphin

This is the eye
that spied on the boy
that squinted in the sunlight
that caught the girl's attention

This is the eye
that saw a show
that winked to a friend
that saw a dolphin
that spied on the boy
that squinted in the sunlight
that caught the girl's attention.

Shannen Brown (10)
Daventry Grange Junior School

Puppy

Meat eater
Race beater
Tree climber
Fast mover
Constant chaser
Human killer
Best player
Puppy.

Bronte Coates (7)
Daventry Grange Junior School

THE RAIN STORM

Down came the rain,
Killing all the ants.
The animals hide for fear of fright,
The sun is covered, the clouds go black,
Silence is the object that is in sight.

Rain comes out like a deadly weapon,
People hide for shade and light,
The rain has gone, the light has come,
The sound of nature has arisen,
The hooting wind,
The singing birds,
The light has come
And all is well,
So pack up your bags for
The storm has gone.

Monica Barmby (10)
Daventry Grange Junior School

DOG

Loud woofer
Bad biter
Swift runner
Shaggy shaker
Loud cryer
Messy eater
Nasty scratcher
Sweet sleeper
Dog.

Rebekah Fenwick (8)
Daventry Grange Junior School

THE SILENT TREATMENT

The whistling of the wind,
The swaying of the trees,
No one gets the silent treatment
As much as me.

The singing of the birds,
The buzzing of the bees,
No one gets the silent treatment
As much as me.

The waving of the grass,
The crunching of the leaves,
No one gets the silent treatment
As much as me.

The whistling of the wind,
The swaying of the trees,
No one feels the silent treatment
As much as me.

Peter Gardner (11)
Daventry Grange Junior School

MOUSE

Fast runner
Cheese nibbler
Quick chewer
Good climber
Far jumper
Loud squeaker
Nest maker
Mouse.

Matthew Langlands
Daventry Grange Junior School

THE READER OF THIS POEM
(Based on 'The Writer Of This Poem' by Roger McGough)

The reader of this poem
Is as bossy as a whistle
As high as a mountain
As sharp as a thistle
As slippery as a fountain

As grumpy as a tree
As scary as a ghost
As buzzy as a bee
As stiff as a post

As loopy as chewing gum
As smelly as a pig's ear
And of course troublesome
As shallow as a pie.

Ashley Newell (10)
Daventry Grange Junior School

ANACONDA

Anaconda
Man eater
Prey catcher
Fast eater
Underwater slitherer
Colossal eater
Sharp looker
Prey surpriser
Soft sneaker
Anaconda.

Jake Tebbutt
Daventry Grange Junior School

THESE ARE THE LIPS

These are the lips
that kissed a boy
and whistled in the wind
that had lipstick on for Saturday night

These are the lips
that talked to my mum
and blew a bubble
they shape my mood

These are the lips
that recite a poem
sing a song
and touch my tongue

These are the lips
that sing a song
blow a bubble
and whistle with the wind
and I will never lose them.

Amelia Spalding (10)
Daventry Grange Junior School

THE SUN IS LIKE . . .

The sun is like a light bulb
that brightens up the sky.
The moon is like a large football
that floats up high.
The trees are like people
swaying in the breeze.
The clouds are like cotton wool
drifting slowly by.

Jo-Ann Goacher (11)
Daventry Grange Junior School

THIS IS THE FOOT

This is the foot
that took possession

This is the foot
that took possession
that kicked the ball

This is the foot
that took possession
that kicked the ball
that tackled Ryan Giggs

This is the foot
that took possession
that kicked the ball
that tackled Ryan Giggs
that became famous

This is the foot
that never got lost.

Kayleigh Muller (9)
Daventry Grange Junior School

THESE ARE THE EYES

These are the eyes
that look for help
that watch the rain
that saw a fish
that cry tears
that wink and blink
and peer round the corner
with a dazzly blue iris
and close at night.

Chloe Stephenson (9)
Daventry Grange Junior School

THIS IS THE ARM

This is the arm
that posses the wrist
which looks after the hand
as if it is ill and sick

This is the arm
that helped raise the child

This is the arm
that's too long to fit
into a knitted jumper

This is the arm
that shot up in anger

This is the arm
that shot up in anger
that is too long to fit into the jumper
that helped raise the child
which looked after the wrist

This is the arm
that never gets lost.

Rebecca Wade (10)
Daventry Grange Junior School

THIS IS THE MOUTH

This is the mouth
that opens wide
that tastes the food
that drinks the juice

This is the mouth
that gulps at night
that keeps my gums warm
that spits the flies

This is the mouth
that covers my teeth
that shakes with sourness
that hums a tune

This is the mouth
that blows a kiss
that blew a bubble
that speaks out loud

This is the mouth
that your tongue lives in
that makes faces.

Amie Billson (9)
Daventry Grange Junior School

THIS IS THE FOOT

This is the foot
that kicked the ball
that scored the goal
that made my toe numb

This is the foot
that helped us win
that helped us win the Premiership
that made us all happy

This is the foot
that broke a toe
that twisted an ankle
and he never played again

This is the foot
that ran into the box
that volleyed a cross
which hit the back of the net

This is the foot
that ran into the box
that broke a toe
that helped us win
that kicked the ball
that won us the game!

Matthew Humphreys (10)
Daventry Grange Junior School

THESE ARE THE EYES

These are the eyes
that watched the show
that saw a dolphin
and a golden tiger

These are the eyes
that saw a box
that is chained
around a fox

These are the eyes
that spied on a girl
that cried some tears
that lost her pearl

These are the eyes
that saw a pool
that had purple water
that was cool

These are the eyes
that saw a strange fight
in a park
over a pint

These are the eyes
that saw a grave
that saw a shark
and a slave

These are the eyes
that saw a dolphin
and a fox
that spied on a girl
saw a pool
a strange fight
and a slave

These are the eyes
that will never get lost.

Kimberley Miller (9)
Daventry Grange Junior School

THE HAUNTED HOUSE

The haunted house is very dark!
So no one goes in there!
Because people say there is something in its lair!
I went in for a dare!
It was spooky there!
No curtains there!
No carpets too!
Don't go in there, I would not dare!
It is a lair!
It is the monster's lair!

Chelsea Thompson (9)
Daventry Grange Junior School

THIS IS THE FOOT

This is the foot
that kicked a ball
jumped over the wall
and had a great fall

This is the foot
that ran a race
just in case
he went into that place

This is the foot
that put on a shoe
don't know how
he doesn't know Sue

This is the foot
that hurt its toe
wore a pink bow
and bought a crow

This is the foot
that never gets lost.

Louise Dyson (10)
Daventry Grange Junior School

WEATHER

Rain is like an enormous tap.
The sun is like a bonfire.
Lightning is like a hammer.
Hailstones are like stones falling.
Snow is like cotton balls falling.

Kieran Cherry (9)
Daventry Grange Junior School

THESE ARE THE FEET

These are the feet that kicked the ball
and scored the goal
which won the Premiership

These are the feet that ran the mile
and came second position

These are the feet that soiled the rug
after crushing the bug

These are the feet that triggered the fall
which made me slip down the hole
but let me see the beautiful foals

These are the feet that saw the foal
made me slip down the hole
crushed the bug, soiled the rug
ran the mile and kicked the ball

These are the feet that hold my trust.

Jonathan Lane (10)
Daventry Grange Junior School

MONKEY

Noisy screamer
Doody jumper
Huge banana eater
Funny squeaker
Nasty nibbler
Cute looker
Amazing swinger
Monkey.

Jodie Bunting
Daventry Grange Junior School

Snow

S   now is very cold
N   o, it can't be sold
O   h, snow is much fun
W   hy does it melt in the sun?

I   like playing in the snow
S   ometimes you can put on a snow show

F   eels soft, it is
U   nder the tree, I sit with fizz
N   o, the snow has gone!

Lauren Aris (8)
Daventry Grange Junior School

I Saw A Monster

One day I saw a monster
It was running down the lane
It looked like it was in pain
I asked him if he was alright
He said, 'I've just been in a fight'
I asked him if he was hungry
He said, 'Yes I am'
So guess who he ate?
Me!

Karen Claydon (9)
Daventry Grange Junior School

THIS IS THE FOOT

This is the foot
that kicked a ball
that broke its toe
that tested the pool

This is the foot
that kicked my brother
that scored a penalty
that kicked a bag

This is the foot
that hid in its shoe
that started bleeding
that squashed a bug

This is the foot
that did some dancing
that won us the World Cup
that scored the winning goal

This is the foot
that kicked a ball
that scored a goal
that hid in its shoe
that did some dancing
that rid a skateboard.

Jordan Timson (10)
Daventry Grange Junior School

THE BATTLEFIELD

The battlefield silent and still,
The deadly weapons at rest,
After the night of the kill.

The ground like a river of blood,
Ripped and torn,
With trenches covered in mud.

Screams of dying no more,
Just the wives weeping of their loses
And crying their eyes out.

The battlefield silent and still,
The deadly weapons at rest,
After the night of the kill.

Stuart Jaeckel (10)
Daventry Grange Junior School

BIG SURPRISE

We're having a party, we're having it for Mum
She's done so much work, she should have a break
Like a little party on Valentine's Day
She'll nearly be here, we better hide,
She's coming, ready to have a jump, ready
She's having a surprise
The door's open, she's having a little fright, ready
1, 2, 3
Surprise!

Joe Osborne (9)
Daventry Grange Junior School

WRITING A POEM IS HARD

I always thought writing a poem was hard,
'Cause I never could write one,
However hard I tried,
Nothing ever came out right.

Until one day in literacy,
I noticed something strange,
A large tick had been planted,
On the poem I had written yesterday.

I thought the teacher had made a mistake,
But when I asked her, she said it was right,
I was so pleased that I've only just realised,
That I can write a poem,
However hard it seems.

Georgina Davies (10)
Daventry Grange Junior School

SNAKE

Skin shedder
Great hisser
Slimy slitherer
Wild hunter
Poisonous tonguer
Meat eater
Ferocious biter
Rat eater
Snake.

Robert Claydon (7)
Daventry Grange Junior School

THE READER OF THIS POEM
(Based on 'The Writer Of This Poem' by Roger McGough)

The reader of this poem is as silly as a clown
as fierce as fire
as cold as ice
as scary as a hippo

As trouble-making as a cat
as full of life as the wind
as jumpy as a ball
as happy as happy can be

The reader of this poem is my friend, Jo.

Shauna Middleton (10)
Daventry Grange Junior School

CATS

Post scratcher
Mice chaser
Fish eater
Fun player
Shy stranger
Quiet purrer
Foot rubber
High pouncer
Cat.

Hayley Duncan (8)
Daventry Grange Junior School

THINK . . .

Think pink
Like the frosting on top of a cake
Think jasmine
Like a fiery chilli pepper
Think . . .

Think indigo
Like the berries in the trees
Think burgundy
Like the crispy bacon burning
Think . . .

Think ochre
Like the corn in a meadow
Think turquoise
Like the shimmer in the sea
Think . . .

Think
Of the swirls of all the colours
Think . . .

Fiona McCance (10)
Daventry Grange Junior School

SNOW

Ice skating, snowboarding, sledging,
Skiing, footprints in the snow.
Glide, skate, skid, slip on old Jack Frost's ice.
All the streams, ponds and rivers freeze,
Joy and laughter fill the air,
Snowflakes sprinkles everywhere.

Tabitha Coates (8)
Daventry Grange Junior School

PUPPY

Fast runner
Hard biter
Post scratcher
Rough player
Slipper chewer
Cat chaser
Meat eater
Good walker
Puppy.

Emma Furnivall (8)
Daventry Grange Junior School

SNAKE

Skin shedder
Smooth slitherer
Killer poisoner
Rat eater
Boa constrictor
Hiss hisser
Fast mover
Snake.

Ryan James (7)
Daventry Grange Junior School

DOG

Bum sniffer
Tail chaser
Face licker
Good player
Loud barker
Fast runner
Skin scratcher
Kennel liver
Dog.

Georgia Wilson (8)
Daventry Grange Junior School

LEOPARD

Spotty camouflager
Best hider
Best pouncer
Good chaser
Super killer
Top hunter
Great sprinter
Speedy runner
Leopard.

Alex Kibblewhite (7)
Daventry Grange Junior School

NIGHT FIRE

At midnight a flash of light,
The air turned so bright.

In the air a flash of fire,
It rises higher and higher.

A bolt of lightning,
It crashes.

It all lit up in a lot of flashes,
Like a lot of whiplashes.

Scott Smith (10)
Daventry Grange Junior School

SNOWFLAKES

Snowflakes are white and sparkly,
They fall silently from the sky.
They feel smooth, fluffy and cold,
In the palm of my hand.

I made a snowman the other day,
But now it's started to melt away!
Never to be seen again,
Gone for good and good for gone!

Shannon Thompson (11)
Daventry Grange Junior School

I WONDER WHAT RED IS?

Red is a blazing traffic light, a sunset of the dawn of dark,
A ripening plum, waiting to be eaten,
Sits in its bowl all dripping and wet,
The poppies in the field, all colours red,
The same red roses dazzling in the sun,
Thinking itself of number one,
Red as a ball bouncing in the midnight sky,
Why was red invented?
Who knows?
Why?

Rhianne Wykes (11)
Daventry Grange Junior School

THE READER OF THIS POEM
(Based on 'The Writer Of This Poem' by Roger McGough)

The reader of this poem is as vicious as a shark
He will rip you to shreds,
He is as angry as a tiger,
He is as bad as a robber,
He'll crush you till you're as thin as a ruler,
He is as scary as a ghost,
He is as sneaky as a spy,
He is as disobedient as a newborn puppy.

Tessa Withall (11)
Daventry Grange Junior School

THE BATTLE OF THE RING

Amongst the hills the castle stands,
Its stone walls, magnificent and grand,
As all around it is open land,
Into the distance the plains expand,
In many tower'd Isengard.
Its ancient bridge spans the moat,
Where all the bodies will bleed and float,
All attackers should take note,
The battle of the ring.

As Aragorn stands tall and proud,
Hear his battle cry, mighty loud,
The rain falls from a darkened cloud,
As the mighty Orc army howled,
In many tower'd Isengard.
The Orcs attacked with mighty power,
Their charge focused upon the tower,
Causing us to hide and cower,
The battle of the ring.

All was lost, all hope was gone,
'Look to the east,' said Aragorn,
We all looked as the sun shone
And there was Gandalf on horse upon,
In many tower'd Isengard.
With word and spell the Orcs were killed
And much blood was lost and spilled,
It was with joy our hearts were filled
The battle of the ring.

Stuart Maxwell (10)
Earls Barton Junior School

WORLD WAR II

The soldiers wait for peace to end
And for the fight 'gainst other men
And in the ward, nurse waits to tend
The wounds of soldiers who will lend
Their lives for power'd England.
Then they charge, ready to kill
German soldiers now, until
They all battle for their country's will,
The fated World War II.

Adolph Hitler, vilest man,
Kills innocent people, because he can
And drops the bombs, the constant bang
Of German missiles, coloured tan,
To take the lives of England.
The troops all kill with guns and shells,
The smoke gives off intensive smells,
Then everyone hears the dreaded bells,
The fated World War II.

The fighting stops, then all is still
And all the soldiers stop the kill,
They suddenly cease of their own free will,
Their leader's suicide on the hill,
Means victory for England.
Adolph Hitler, dead and gone,
Everyone knows what he has done,
He's given up the German gun
And ended World War II.

Sam Homer (10)
Earls Barton Junior School

WAITING

I'm waiting by the bedside,
Looking for a sign,
My mum and dad keep saying
That everything will be fine.

That car crash seemed so sudden,
There was nothing I could do,
Grandad just lying there
And me screaming for Auntie Sue.

Tomorrow's the operation,
Aunt Sue's losing it a bit,
We're praying Grandad'll get through,
He's always been healthy and fit.

Joanne Taylor (10)
Great Addington CE Primary School

PLAYGROUND

I'm sitting on the bench,
No one to talk to,
It's always like this,
Waiting for a friend, but who?

People passing,
In gangs and groups,
My eyes are filling with tears,
I wish I was one of them in a big happy group.

Alex Page (10)
Great Addington CE Primary School

CHOCOLATE

Chocolate is my favourite thing,
But sometimes people don't tuck in.
Me and chocolate will stick together,
Our friendship will last forever!

Charlotte Evans (10)
Great Addington CE Primary School

BROTHER

I have a little brother
Who is much more than a pest,
He mainly is shouting,
His lips are always pouting!

Jack is annoying on the computer,
Jack is annoying when we're at school,
Jack is annoying when he takes my micro-scooter!
I wish Jack wasn't annoying at all.

Naomi Brown (9)
Great Addington CE Primary School

SOFTWARE

The computer is the thing for me,
It keeps me busy and studious.
A hand from my dad is really great,
It's fun and marvellous.

Jamie Vendy (11)
Great Addington CE Primary School

SEASIDE

All across the beach,
All across the shore,
Little children playing as it was before.

Mums and dads relaxing,
Watching children run,
All getting a tan by the midday sun.

The sun is going down,
It's time to go home,
The seagulls fly away all alone.

Annabelle Chang (10)
Great Addington CE Primary School

FOLLOWING THE DEATH OF A PET

I am sitting here all alone
Waiting to see if he's dead
My dad brings him out
I can just see his head

I started to cry
I ran to my room
My dad followed me
Why did he have to die so soon?

Chloe Brudenell (10)
Great Addington CE Primary School

WATERFALL

A shower of secrets,
plunging like rainbows,
to the frothing, foaming, unknown depths
of the mysterious pool below.

Down, down, down they go,
through the murmuring sound of trees,
exploring everything.

Antonia Brown (11)
Great Addington CE Primary School

WILD

In the savannah and in the air,
Some in the water so beware,
Elephants stomp all over the place,
Watch the lion and zebra chase.

Climb a tree away from the ground,
Be quiet, *ssh!* Don't make a sound.
Swim with dolphins, dive down deep,
Cartwheel, back flips, see them leap!

See the panda eat bamboo,
Yum-yum, chew, chew.
Jungle creatures creep and crawl,
All for one and one for all!

Esther Allen (10)
Great Addington CE Primary School

HURRICANE

A hurricane is coming,
A hurricane is coming,
Run for your lives,
Run for your lives.

Smashing up the town,
Destroying our homes,
Everything is ruined,
When will it stop?

A hurricane is coming,
A hurricane is coming,
Run for your lives,
Run for your lives.

No school, no work,
Everyone is hiding,
Everything is flying,
Babies are crying.

A hurricane is coming,
A hurricane is coming,
Run for your lives,
Run for your lives.

Trees in the air,
This isn't fair,
A terrifying sight.

Jonathan Bowater (10)
Great Addington CE Primary School

THE SEA

The sea is a fierce wolf
Big and grey
He pounces up and down each day
With his scruffy fur and his jagged teeth
Hour upon hour he cries
The screeching, piercing sound
Echoes all around
Of bones, bones, bones, bones
The giant sea-wolf moans
Licking his greasy paws
And when the night wind roars
He props himself up on his claws
And howls, howls, howls, howls.

Stephanie Langford (9)
Long Buckby Junior School

THE CLOUD IS A . . .

The cloud is a big sheep, fluffy and white
You can't see it that well at night
With its soft touch and fluff
The cloud is not very tough

A big white sheep and a big fluffy coat
The cloud is so quiet, you can't hear a thing
But when it is storming
You can hear something.

Mary-Anne Blowman (9)
Long Buckby Junior School

KING OF LOVE LAND

He flew in a teapot through candyfloss clouds,
The sun was heart-shaped and pink,
The colourful birds flew all around
And sparkling fish jumped into the rainbow river.

He landed on spiky fish,
He met a heart-shaped person.
He walked on heart-shaped stones,
He went to a heart-shaped wedding.

The king said to the heart-shaped person, 'Congratulations.'
The heart-shaped person said, 'Thank you.'
So he had a drink of red champagne,
He went to bed on a bed of hearts.

In the morning he got his teapot out,
Said, 'Thanks' to the heart-shaped man,
He flew away through candyfloss clouds and the gooey sun,
He was soon back at his island.

Sophie Humphries (8)
Long Buckby Junior School

THE RED KITE

Curving claws grasp the mountain's peak;
Twisting his head holding piercing eyes, and yet,
Clasping every darting motion . . .
in his mind.
As though in agitation,
he dashes speedily towards the dark, dismal clouds,
yet –
like a burning ball of bronze feathers,
he swoops.
Plummeting down in a vicious advance,
eyeing prey of taste
and now he's approaching, silently,
to snatch his prey.
Hovering above loudly rustling pines,
he must not miss this opportunity
to kill.
Now! He strikes!
Grasping catch in his
lethal,
retracting,
claws.

Natalie Price (9)
Long Buckby Junior School

A SUMMER DAY

A summer morning when the sun is shining,
Birds are singing in the summer breeze,
The dogs are lying on the warm summer grass,
Forgotten is the winter's freeze.

People swimming through the salty sea,
Dolphins jumping through the waves,
Fish free-wheeling in the warm seawater,
Seals lying in the caves.

Hundreds of ice creams being bought,
Lollies being licked by the score,
Cold drinks being sipped all day,
As the heat burns more and more.

Turtles swim round and round,
Crabs scuttle across the sandy bay,
Children leap over waves
And sea horses loll about all day.

Emma Gradwell (10)
Long Buckby Junior School

FUN AT THE FAIR

Wibble wobble wibble wobble
On the bouncy castle

Bump boom bish bash
In the dark green dodgems

Splish splosh splash slush
Sliding down the water chute

Twisting twirling twisting twirling
Snaking round the roller coaster

Screaming creeping screaming creeping
Spooked in the haunted house

Win a prize, win a prize
Try your luck on hook-a-duck

Back and forth, back and forth
Swinging on the swings

Spin and spin round and round
Get dizzy on the roundabout

Bounce and bounce up and down
Trampolines are fun

Churning tummy, feeling sick
Too much candyfloss, let's go home.

Bethany Duffin (8)
Long Buckby Junior School

THERE'S A WAR

There's a war going on in my head,
Everywhere I go, it's raging, whatever good times I have,
It's hanging over me like a huge shadow, blocking out the sun.
Planes fly over, women and children cry, and . . . that's it.
Many people will not see the new day dawn.
A few words out of a politician's mouth, that's all it takes!
There are a few unanswered questions that drive me out of my mind:
What is the point of killing harmless people
Just for some other people's disagreements?
Why does the world stand for violence and cruelty, and most of all,
Who is to be blamed?
When I go to bed at night, I sometimes have nightmares,
But these are not about ghosts and vampires,
I dream that I'm in Iraq, watching the troops come closer
With every sunrise.
Then I wake up and remember I'm in England, safe.
Whoever reads this may think I am odd,
But just remember that it could happen to you.

Daisy Woolham (10)
Long Buckby Junior School

THE SUMMER POEM

Listen
It is summer
Children playing outside
See the sun in the sky
Shining.

Ruwaydah Mauderbux (8)
Rockingham Primary School

FLOWERS - CINQUAIN

Look, look!
See the flowers
Growing by the roses
The daffodils growing yellow
By day.

Jordan Lee Clough (9)
Rockingham Primary School

DOGS - CINQUAIN

The dogs
They're man's best friend
They will fetch the paper
Dogs always chase the cats around
The dogs.

Mark Stewart (8)
Rockingham Primary School

CATS - CINQUAIN

My cat
Is beautiful
Warm and fast, black and white
She is the best ever around
This street.

Jake Bettles (9)
Rockingham Primary School

BROTHERS - CINQUAIN

Brothers
Pains in the neck
Rampage through your room
Hate mostly everything you like
Hate 'em.

Anthony Flude Bailey-Grice (9)
Rockingham Primary School

NOISES - CINQUAIN

Listen
Hear the echo
Of the sweet singing birds
Calling to their next-door neighbours
Sweetly.

Sarah McNamee (8)
Rockingham Primary School

SUN OF MINE - CINQUAIN

Maybe
The sun will come
Out of the dull dark sky
I hope people will like that sun
Of mine.

Abigail Hardy (8)
Rockingham Primary School

SUMMER PLAY - CINQUAIN

Summer
It is the time
To go and play today
Tim and Jack want to play with you
That's cool.

Paige Stewart (9)
Rockingham Primary School

WIND - CINQUAIN

Listen
To the soft wind
Blowing in the sunlight
Making clouds blow around the world
Gently.

Sarah Baird (9)
Rockingham Primary School

NATURE - CINQUAIN

Listen
Can you hear trees
Move in the shade of dark
When ants start to move, then they groove
Up trees.

Luke Stimson (9)
Rockingham Primary School

SPRING FLOWERS - CINQUAIN

Look now
Smell the blossom
Daffodils bow proudly
All the flowers sway in the breeze
Quickly.

Rebecca Liquorish (9)
Rockingham Primary School

AUTUMN

Listen
For rustling
In the bushes near
Is it a fox?
Is it a wolf
Waiting?

Bryn Williams (8)
Rockingham Primary School

SPRINGTIME - CINQUAIN

Listen
To the birds tweet
The daffodils are sweet
Listen to the dogs bark quietly
Listen.

Sean King (9)
Rockingham Primary School

FAMILY - CINQUAIN

Morning
I just got up
Mum's setting the breakfast
Dad's in a tizzy on the stairs
Oh school!

Chelsea Towers (9)
Rockingham Primary School

MONDAY - CINQUAIN

Monday
I'm to get up
Dad is in a hurry
Mum is still not up yet, lazy
School time!

Taylor Booth (8)
Rockingham Primary School

STRONG WIND - CINQUAIN

Listen
To the strong wind
Blowing the leaves around
Icy leaves are frosty and crisp
On ground.

Hannah Alcorn (8)
Rockingham Primary School

THE SEASIDE - CINQUAIN

Summer
Sun is shining
The sand below our feet
The sea is freezing cold today
Jump in!

Philip Cain (8)
Rockingham Primary School

A BRAND NEW DAY - CINQUAIN

Morning
Sun rising high
Bright refreshing new day
Though soon it turns to night-time once
Again.

Drew Ramsay (9)
Rockingham Primary School

PEACE - CINQUAIN

Listen
Peace in nature
No more hunting today
Foxes in their den waiting for
Some food.

Aaron McCabe (8)
Rockingham Primary School

Starlight In Summer - Cinquains

Listen
The wild dogs howl
Whispers all around us
Stars are shining brightly above
Quiet

Summer
It's time to play
Time to run in the breeze
It's another summer's day in
Fresh air.

Sophie Hughes (8)
Rockingham Primary School

Family

Families are fun,
My mum gives me a bun.
My brother pretends to shoot me with his toy gun.
My dad collects the water from the well,
I help him load the buckets onto the oxes.
My sister,
Well I'll tell you how many toys she has . . .
One hundred boxes.

Alys Winter (9)
Rowlett CP School

THE LAST DAY AT SCHOOL

I look at the school
The classrooms and the swimming pool
I sit in my chair
Not much longer I'll be sitting there
My friends will miss me, I hope they don't kiss me
I see mine and my friends' drawers
I see all the snack food
The cups and the straws

I look at my books
It'll be my last looks
At the school
I look at my teacher's stool
I look at the board
And my friend playing with a pretend sword
I say goodbye
I start to cry
I wipe my eyes
I won't have to wear these horrible school ties.

Amber Hendry (10)
Rowlett CP School

THE OLD MAN FROM PENZANCE

There was an old man from Penzance
Who sold rather large smelly pants
But he started to prance
But went off in a trance
That old man from Penzance.

Oscar Winter (10)
Rowlett CP School

In Trouble

Opened the door
Sat in my chair
I look at her
I dare not stare

I sit there silent
She looks at me mad
It was a mistake
Yesterday I was bad

I smashed a window
With my ball
I hit the window
In the hall

My blood boils
I start to sweat
I really wish
I could just forget

She tells me to stand up
Some people start to stare
She tells me to go to the head teacher
Oh Miss, that is not very fair

I stand at the door
He looks down to me, he's very tall
I start to sweat, I just confess
I smashed the window in the hall.

Paige Gibson (10)
Rowlett CP School

FISHING

When I went fishing
I was wishing
That I could catch a fish
Then put it on a dish
And give it to my cat
On her mat
She will eat it down
Like a clown
She makes me laugh
She is daft.

Carl Page (10)
Rowlett CP School

MY BOY

My boy, Dale
Is the eldest of four
He gets no peace from anyone
Dale helps around the house
And helps others in their need
But most of all, he has so much love
To share with everyone.

Dale Page (10)
Rowlett CP School

IN TROUBLE!

As I run
Through the street
I feel the blood
Run to my feet

I hear the dogs
Run after me
Chasing
As I try to flee

The shopkeeper pounces
He grabs the air
Just misses me
By a hair

The police are now
On the case
The sweat is
Running down my face

I'm ready to
Turn around and confess
But it will make my
Life an utter mess!

The police are near
I haven't any puff
The road is
Starting to get rough

OK, I confess
My heart starts to ping
I stole
The diamond ring.

Marie Elliott & Scot Gilhespie (11)
Rowlett CP School

THE LAST DAY AT SCHOOL

I look at the school
I look at the place
My eyes are crying
My tears burn my face

I look around
Whilst I sit on my chair
People are watching
They start to stare

I miss my teachers
And my friends
I hope I'll see them again
I hope this isn't the end

My classroom fades
As I walk away
I wish and wish
I could stay

It's time to go
It's not that fun
See you sometime
But now it's over and done.

Carly Devlin (9) & Georgia Dewar (10)
Rowlett CP School